ANDROID

Keeping You Secure

David Lyon

Copyright, Disclaimer and Trademarks

Contents

Introduction

My name is David Lyon and I am a security professional. I am a Certified Information Systems Security Professional and have been working professionally in the information technology (IT) field for more than 10 years. My professional experience has included healthcare, education, Department of Defense contractors and even a two-employee business. I have always been the 'go-to' person for all things technology and security with my friends, family and coworkers. While not working, I enjoy tinkering with my various cars, doing home improvement projects and trying out new recipes for different types of food.

I promise to use this book to teach you as much as possible on the topic covered.

I also promise not to hold back and 'beat around the bush'. You may not agree with everything I say, and that's OK, but I will tell you what I know from experience, research and my general knowledge of the IT and security world.

Please let me know if you find any errors or have any comments on the topic of this book.

Piracy

While I would hope everyone who reads this book has purchased it legitimately, I know that's far from reality. If you have downloaded a copy of this book from somewhere besides Amazon, all I ask is you review the book. Please write your review on either Amazon or Goodreads to help others find my books.

Standards and Notes

While writing this book, there are several standards I like to follow for formatting.

Complicated links are shortened using Google's goo.gl link creator. Amazon links will be shortened using their link creator. This will ease visiting the links mentioned. I know it can be tough to follow links from an eBook or paper copy, but these links should help. They are case sensitive and are followed by a description of where the link will take you (e.g. Amazon.com).

To draw more attention to certain items, I will use the following icons.

 Information to take note of is designated with this pencil icon.

 When some information or action requires more caution, this icon will be used.

 This icon will allow you to further explore the topic covered with sources and search terms.

Why is Security Important for Android?

Android is the world's most popular mobile operating system; why is it that important to keep yourself secure?

Your smart phone is now arguably the most important computing devices that you now own.
Do you receive email on your device?
Are you connected to various social networking accounts?
Do you have private conversations and text messages on your device?
Or pictures you wouldn't want to share with the world?
How about banking applications; do you use them?

If you think "I've got nothing to hide" or that you have nothing of interest to a hacker, you're wrong. Hackers come in all shapes, sizes and motivations. You may not be a target of state agencies, but some teenager who is just cutting his teeth in the hacking world may see you as the prize of their beginning hacking life. Your misery would be their bragging rights to other hackers and friends.

Don't become a statistic on privacy and hacking.

Smart phones are becoming more and more the only device people use. Some people even believe that the applications they use on their phones are 'the internet' and no longer use a web browser.

 http://goo.gl/fzDp1P (Device Atlas) – Some interesting statistics on smart phone usage in 2016.

What would you do if your phone was compromised and a hacker gained access to all information linked to that device?

What if someone was able to lock you out of your email?
Hackers could likely gain access to any account that uses your email address

to reset its password. Can you reset your bank account information with just your current email address? Maybe, maybe not, but would a hacker be able to reset it with all the information in your email and applications linked to on your smartphone? Very likely.

So the simple answer to why it's important to secure your device is: To protect yourself, your information, your family's information and your livelihood.

According to the U.S Department of Justice, the average financial loss per identity theft incident is $4,930. These victims spend an average of $851 to $1378 in expenses related to their cases. (Source: https://goo.gl/RcC1IE WrightUSA.com)

This all may seem very doom and gloom, but please, just take a few moments to follow the steps in this book and help protect yourself from the very real possibility of loss.

Update Your Device

My personal 'rule number one' of protecting any information system — run system updates. It's the first thing I do when setting up a new computer or buying any new electronic device. These updates are available because someone has found a flaw, bug or vulnerability in the system you just turned on.

Maybe you've run into this situation before? You get this brand new, fancy, top-of-the-line device home, plug it in, and BAM! Updates. Ugh! What a huge headache!

Sure, updates seem like a hassle, and who really wants to update? It never fails, every time I turn on my PlayStation and attempt to play a game there are several updates waiting for me. These updates are extremely important and on some systems, like the PlayStation, are required before you can even use the system online.

Android is in a rather unique situation for updates. The Android landscape is full of different manufacturers, different networks and a wide variety of versions. At the time of this writing, the latest version of Android available to the general public is 7.0.x. Google has begun releasing monthly security updates for select devices that are extremely important to the security of your device.

Here's how to check your Android version:

Go to your *Settings* screen, pictured below. Keep in mind these screen shots are from Android version 6.0.1, your device may look different. Often times *Settings* can be found in the All Apps section of the device, which is the bottom middle button on the main screen.

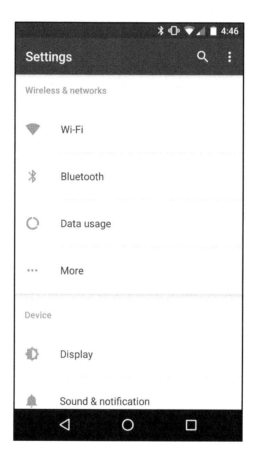

After opening *Settings,* scroll to the very bottom and tap on *About phone.*

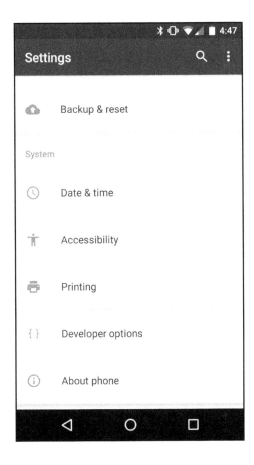

The version of the device will be displayed on the next screen, similar to the screen shot below.

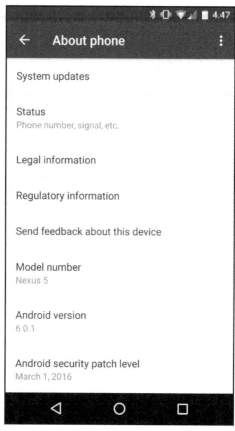

What version of Android is your device running? Unfortunately, unless your device is brand new, your answer is not likely 6.0.1 (or later). If you have a newer device, and you're not at the latest version, you can try to use the *System updates* feature at the top of that previous screen shot. It may have an update waiting for you. I would recommend installing any updates available.

So you don't have the latest version, what can you possibly do to update your Android operating system? I hate to be the bearer of bad news, but likely nothing with your existing phone. Most manufacturers of Android devices release their newest model and then forget about them. It makes manufacturers more money to keep pumping out new smart phones with slightly bigger screens, better cameras, and different features than it does to keep their past devices updated.

Manufacturers aren't the only at fault, even the carriers shoulder some of this blame. The problem really lies in the tweaks and modifications that carriers and manufacturers make to the Android operating system software when they install it on their devices. These tweaks and modifications include their built in programs, visual improvements and menu changes. Google can't install updates to modified Android devices because it may break these extras.

I will admit, I have been an Android customer since I could afford to buy a smart phone. I started with the HTC Evo 4G, went to a Motorola Photon 4G, improved with a Samsung Galaxy Nexus and am now using a LG Nexus 5. Far and away the best phone of the group has been the Nexus 5. The Nexus name is used on phones that are designed and produced for/by Google. With the next version of Google's phone line, they are dropping the 'Nexus' name and will be using 'Pixel'. Since the Nexus 4, these phones have been the fastest to receive updates, have been properly maintained (with updates) by Google and are by far the best Android phones because of their support.

"But David!" you may say "My Samsung/LG/Motorola so-and-so is the best smart phone because of this awesome feature!"

Some of these Nexus phones may not have the most whiz-bang features and nifty gadgets that others have, but they receive direct updates and support from Google. And since we're focusing on security, this support is key to your data and device's security.

Back to the main point, if your phone is on the latest and greatest Android version now, congratulations! Someday in the future you may need this information again. If you aren't on the latest, don't hold your breath for an update, take it in to your own hands. The easiest (and best) way to update is to purchase a new Nexus/Pixel device.

 Nexus devices can be purchased directly from the Google Play store. https://store.google.com/ If the link no longer works, search with Google for "Google Play Store Nexus Devices" or "Google Play Store Pixel Devices".

At time of publication, there are two current models of Nexus devices, the Nexus 5X and Nexus 6P. The numbers roughly reference the size of the screen. For a good all-around phone, the Nexus 5X is more than enough. If big and powerful is more your style, the 6P would be your device. These phones were both released in late 2015, and based on Google's update history, should receive updates for the next 2-3 years. New Google branded devices are expected in October of 2016.

You should not use a device past its supported life which usually ends when it stops receiving security updates. My Nexus 5 is coming towards end-of-life and I will likely have 3-6 months before I am forced to replace it. This is the cost of having such a fancy device, that contains so much personal information, for making phone calls. It really is a full featured computer in your hand.

For best security, you should plan to upgrade your phone about every 2-3 years with a new Nexus (or Pixel) device. These phones can be put on nearly any network (AT&T, Sprint, T-Mobile, Verizon, etc.) and you can even use them on prepaid services and discounted phone plans.

Even if you don't upgrade your smart phone, most of the security steps after this chapter do not require the latest version of Android.

Use a Strong Lock Screen

After updates, the most important step to secure your phone is setting a strong lock screen password. Lock screens protect your data if your device is lost or stolen. According to a national survey, smart phone theft is on the decline, but these numbers still are quite amazing http://goo.gl/d1kG6Q (Consumer Reports). A Consumer Reports survey published in June of 2015 shows that 2.1 million Americans had their phones stolen and another 3.1 million phones were lost in the last year. This data is from June 2014 to June 2015.

So what happens with the devices that are lost and stolen? Is your data still safe? Unless your smart phone is protected, the answer is no. While most stolen phones are erased, then sold for parts, it is still important to secure your data so it doesn't fall in to the wrong hands. This protection is easily obtained on your Android device with the easy steps below.

 Setting a lock screen on your device is **required** for many of the other security measures mentioned in this book.

Tap on the All Apps button and go to *Settings.*
Scroll down to the *Personal* section and tap *Security.*

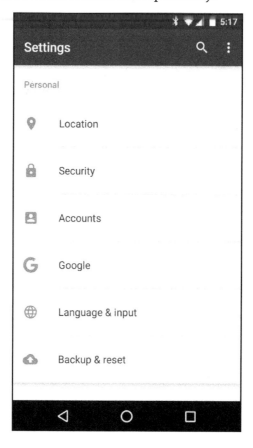

Once you're in the *Security* screen, it should look similar to this. Reminder: This is Android version 6.0.1.

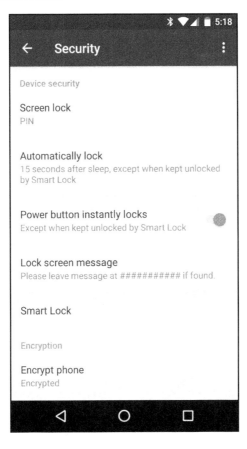

The first option under *Device Security* is the *Screen Lock*. I would recommend at the minimum a PIN. The longer the PIN, the better. Your options are below.

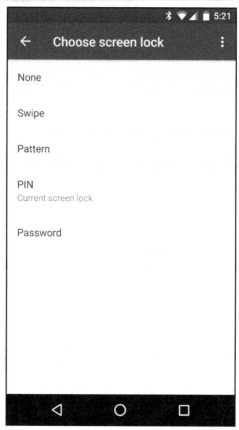

None: Obviously not an option since we're talking security. Anyone turning on your phone will be able to access it.

Swipe: No security gained from this selection. Swiping your finger across the screen will unlock your phone. Please don't use this option or *None*.

Pattern: Better, but still not a great option. You draw a pattern on the screen with your finger to unlock your screen. This is the minimum level of security required for other security features in future chapters.

PIN: This is my recommended minimum option to protect your phone. I currently use PIN and would recommend no less than 6-8 digits.

Password: The best protection. You get a full keyboard option when unlocking your phone. This can be quite a hassle when you need to unlock quickly, but is the best option for security.

Select one of these options. If you already have a lock screen set, you will have to confirm the current password to change to a new setting.

After you have set your Pattern, PIN or Password, you will be asked if you would like to enable *Secure start-up*. *Secure start-up* requires you enter your chosen lock method before the phone will turn on. I would recommend this setting be enabled. Once complete, you are returned to the Security screen.

The next option is *Automatically Lock*. This option forces you to enter your chosen lock method after the screen has turned off from inactivity.

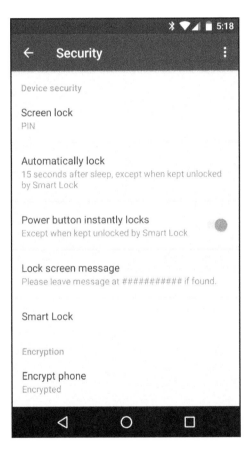

I would recommend setting the Automatic lock time for a short period of time and learning to unlock your device with your chosen lock method. If your device was stolen they would have access for this period of time. Any time limit greater than 1-2 minutes I would not consider secure.

The next toggle on the Security screen is *Power button instantly locks*. This is best set to *On*. If someone were to attempt to steal your device, hitting the power button will lock the screen and require your unlock method.

Moving down, the next field is the *Lock screen message*. This will allow you to give someone who may find your phone helpful information to contact you. For instance, I have brief instructions, an alternate phone number and my name. Since a larger majority of phones are lost rather than stolen, I'd like to give enough information for someone to return my device. This message will also show up on the encryption start screen.

Smart lock is the next feature, which allows you to bypass the lock screen in certain situations. Be careful with these options.

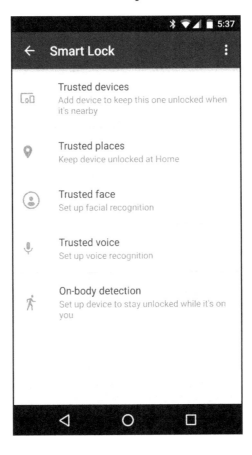

Trusted devices: Allows your Android device to remain unlocked when connected to another Bluetooth device. An example is the Bluetooth in your car stereo system. Your device could remain unlocked when they are paired. Never set this trusted device to be something that can be stolen easily. If someone were to steal a bag or purse that had both devices, your phone would be unlocked as long the paired devices were charged and near each other.

Trusted places: Keeps your device unlocked at specific addresses and places. These can be defined by GPS or address. The radius for this lock is 80 meters which is approximately 262 feet. This is a good option for those who live in areas where the homes are spaced apart, but is not a good option if you live in an apartment building or other close quarters.

Trusted face: Requires you to look at your device's camera for it to unlock. I don't recommend this option as anyone who has similar facial features can unlock your phone. Even Google has this comment: "**IMPORTANT:** This is less secure than a pattern, PIN, or password. Someone who looks similar to you could unlock your phone."

Trusted voice: Uses your voice and the phrase "OK Google" to unlock your device when your voice pattern matches the recorded sample. I do not recommend this option. While Google's voice recognition is good, I wouldn't trust my data to their software.

On-body detection: Works by detecting if you are walking and have the phone vertically placed on your body. It should sense when you set the phone down or sit down and lock. This is hardly a security feature and Google also mentions this in their documentation.

> "**IMPORTANT:** On-body detection may not always be able to tell whose body is connected to on-body detection. If you give your device to someone else while it's unlocked, your device may stay unlocked using on-body detection. Keep in mind that on-body detection as a security feature is less secure than a pattern, PIN, or password. Someone who takes your phone while it's unlocked with on-body detection could access it."

These types of statements should make you think twice about using these features.

Not all of these security features are available on all devices, but if your Android device is updated or you have a Nexus device, you will be able to pick and choose most of them.

Encrypt Your Device

Encryption protects your data by storing it in a scrambled format when your device is powered off. The key to unscramble your data is your lock screen code. Encryption will help prevent someone who has stolen or found your phone from connecting it to their computer and taking your data and pictures. This, combined with a strong screen lock, will keep most thieves from accessing your data.

From the Settings, Security screen, the option *Encrypt phone* is located below.

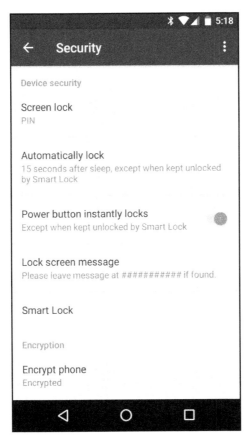

If the device shows anything except "Encrypted" as the current setting, please select the *Encrypt phone/tablet* option.

 This is an irreversible process. There is no 'unencrypt' button or option. The only way back is a factory reset! I still consider this a **very important** step to protecting your phone's data.

Encrypting your phone may take an hour or more. Do not start this process unless you are sure you won't be using your phone for that period of time.

Plug in your device before starting. The device won't start the encryption process unless you're at a certain battery level (80% or higher).

 A Pattern, PIN or password is required before encrypting your phone. It will be your login password when turning on your phone. Don't lose or forget it!

Some older phones, notably anything released prior to Android version 5.0, may suffer from slowed performance with encryption. Newer phones will likely not experience this problem.

After your phone has been encrypted, you will be greeted with this lock screen when booting from an off state.

This screen shows why it's very important to have a good lock screen message. Without it, there would be no information supplied to a good Samaritan looking to return your device.

Enter your Pattern, PIN or Password and your device will continue to boot to the main screen. Congratulations! Your phone is now encrypted!

Use Encrypted Text Messaging

This section deviates from the security of your Android device to security best practices for your data.

Text messaging is one of the most popular methods to communicate. It would make sense to protect that information as well as your device.

Standard Short Messaging Service (SMS) over the phone system can be extremely insecure. Think of it as someone sending you a postcard with seemingly private messages. Everyone at the post office can read this card, and if it were to get misdirected or read in-route, it would be easily read even accidently.

This vulnerability is especially prevalent in older versions of Android. http://goo.gl/v8g97x (ThreatPost.com, 2016)

How can you protect your information sent through text messages? I suggest using any number of these alternative messaging services. Please note: All of these services are only as good as the security settings you place on the account used.

Google Hangouts is my favorite. Since you will set up two factor authentication on your Google account later in this book, this is a no brainer. If your friends have Google Accounts, send them messages in network and all your chats are saved behind a wall of Google security. Now might be a good time to show your friends the chapter on Two Factor Authentication so their account can't be breached easily either.

Facebook Messenger is another widely used messaging service. They advertised recently having over 1 billion users on the Facebook Messenger application. We'll cover Facebook security in another book.

WhatsApp. This is now a Facebook application, but it does employ end-to-end encryption. What does that mean? End-to-end encryption means that the text of your messages is encrypted and unreadable to everyone except the sender and receiver. Even Whatsapp doesn't know what your messages say.

What do all these services have in common? They use the internet instead of the Plain Old Telephone System for the transmission of information. POTS as it's abbreviated, was never designed with security in mind so until phone calls and text messages are encrypted, it's not going to get better.

There are more services than I can list, but these are my top three for Android. While the security they offer is good, likely you will have to convince your friends to install these apps to communicate with them. Text messaging may be unavoidable in some circumstances, but don't use it for anything sensitive.

Enable Android Device Manager

Android Device Manager is another security feature that uses the built in GPS and security features of Android to allow you to ring (locate), lock or erase your device from any web browser. Android Device Manager gives you the ability to locate your device, if lost or stolen, or delete all data to truly ensure your data doesn't end up in the wrong hands.

There are a few prerequisites to using Android Device Manager on your phone.

You must be logged in to your Google Account from your device. Do you have your Gmail account setup on the device? Can you use the Play Store to download applications? If you can do either of these, you are logged in. Your version of Android must support Android Device Manager. It currently supports Android 2.3 and up. You're covered unless your phone came out before December of 2010.

From your Android Device

Earlier versions of Android may require an application installed from the Google Play Store called "Android Device Manager". After install, use that installed application for the settings below.

For later versions of Android, follow the directions below.
On your Android device, navigate to the *Settings* application.
Scroll to the *Google* section.

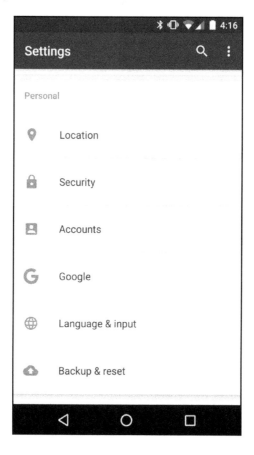

Continue scrolling to near the bottom, a menu called *Security*.

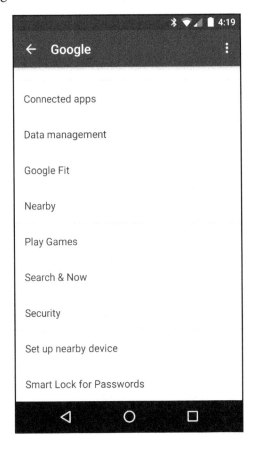

The first two options on this page are used for Android Device Manager.

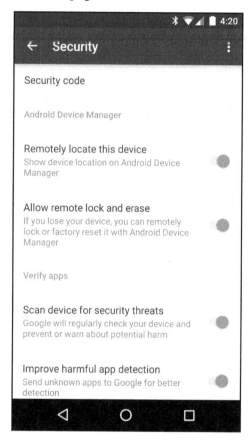

Remotely locate this device allows you to use the Android Device Manager website to find the device using GPS. This would be useful if you lost your phone and would like to know its location.

Allow remote lock and erase lets you to the Google Device Manager website to remotely lock or erase your device. Both options are explained in more detail in the next section.

From Your Web Browser on your Computer

Once you've set up the device manager, you can test it out by navigating to the web site: Android.com/devicemanager

The page displays a Google map view of your phone's location with several options shown below.

Ring: Turns on your device's ringer at maximum volume for 5 minutes or until the power button is pushed. This option doesn't call your device; it just turns on the ringer. Good for finding your device lost in the couch cushions.

Lock: Allow you to lock the device and change the password on the lock screen. This will enable you to set a recovery message and a phone number that can be called from the device. These settings will allow someone who has found your device and would like to return it, the ability to contact you.

Erase: Deletes all the data on the device and performs a factory reset. Be careful with this function as it will disable Android Device Manager because your Google account will no longer be linked to the device. If you chose this option, you will no longer have the ability to locate, ring or lock the device. I would consider this option a last resort to protect your data when you cannot locate or recover your device.

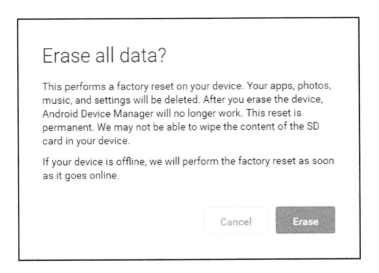

Manage Your Application List

Applications installed on Android require permissions to perform certain functions. For instance, if you're using an email application, it would need access to the internet to receive your mail. An application that manages your contacts would need access to your contact list, and so on.

It's extremely important to be careful where you download applications from and to occasionally prune out ones you are no longer using.

Never download applications from outside the Google Play Store.

This is extremely important since applications outside the Google Play Store do not have to go through the same security checks like those available in the store. This doesn't mean that all Applications in the Play store are safe, but you're more likely secure using them. My hint: if an app has no reviews in the Play Store or the reviews appear generic, avoid it!

 Never install an application from outside the Google Play Store. The Google Play Store acts as your virus scanner and can protect your device if an application is found to be malicious. A majority of Android malware comes from applications installed outside the Google Play Store.

When using Android 6.0 and later, applications prompt you for certain permissions when they first start. This is your second opportunity to read what permissions the application is requesting. The first opportunity is presented when you confirm to install an application from the Google Play Store. Denying access to certain permissions may have an impact on the application's function. You certainly couldn't deny contact access to that contact manager and expect it to work properly.

Want to view installed application permissions?

Navigate to *Settings, Apps* and tap any application. This will show that specific app's permissions. aCar is a great vehicle cost tracking software and as you can see below, it can find my location (for linking local gas stations) and has access to the storage space on my phone (to save its data file).

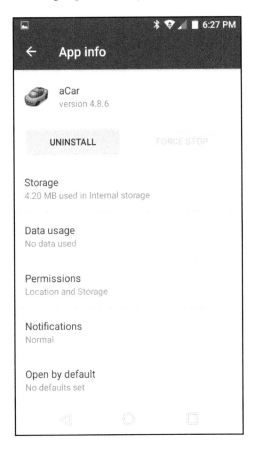

Want to view all permissions?

From the previous Apps list, tap the gear, then go to *App Permissions*. This will show all the permissions types and the list of applications allowed to each.

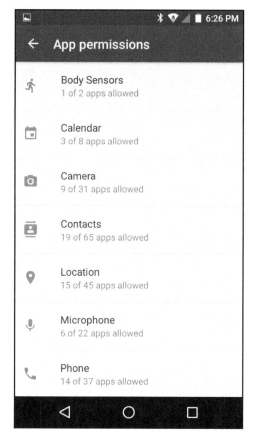

Tapping on any of those permissions allows you to turn on or off permissions for individual apps.

 Turning off permissions for applications may reduce their functionality or break applications. Test your changes by turning off permissions and running the application. You can always come back to this screen to re-enable permissions.

Delete applications you're not using regularly.

Again, navigate to *Settings, Apps* and tap on any specific application. If one of the buttons is "Uninstall" near the top, you can remove the application. If there is a button named Disable in its place, it is likely a built in application. Below is an example, Netflix, which I installed. Since I installed it, it can be uninstalled.

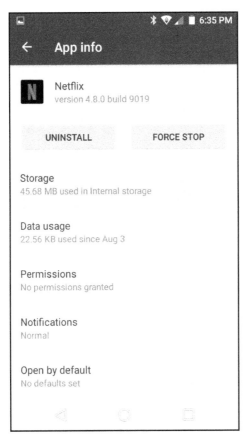

Removing these applications is important to keep your phone running quickly and to stop any that run in the background. Any application that gives you push notifications is likely running in the background now. A push notification is the icon or alert that appears on the top notification bar on your screen. The notification bar is where your time and wireless signal strength appear when your device is unlocked.

Manage Your Wireless Connections

This section focused mainly on the protection of your data and will cover Android specific wireless security as well as some tips for all devices.

You can manage your wireless network connections from the Settings menu.

Open the *Settings* menu from the application list or pull down menu. Tap *Wi-Fi*.

Ensure Wireless is turned *on,* and it should show a list of networks that are currently in range.

Tap the *settings* (three dots) in the top right and go to *Saved networks.*

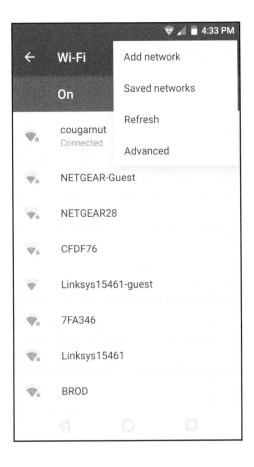

A list of saved networks will display, tap any and click *Forget* from the popup.

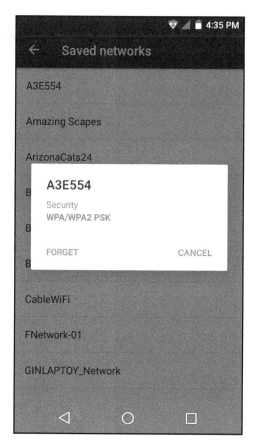

My recommendation is to remove any networks that you don't recognize or don't visit regularly. Coffee shops, electronic stores, grocery stores and more now all offer wireless networks. It seems like everywhere you go, "Free WiFi" is offered so you can quickly get connected to the web. I recommend the deletion of these saved wireless networks from your device so you're not automatically connected when you walk in to your favorite coffee shop or grocery store. Generally, anything you transmit over the air on these networks can be intercepted.

Head back to the *Wi-Fi* screen and tap the menu button and go to *Advanced*.

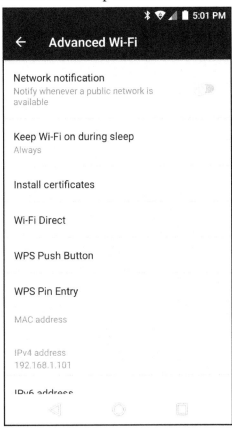

These settings deal more with the operation of the wireless on your device than its security, but while we're in the wireless menu they are worth pointing out.

Network notification allows you to turn on or off the icon that displays in the notification bar when you're in range of an open wireless network.

Scanning always available (not pictured) lets applications check wireless networks to better determine your location when wireless is off.

If you travel and use wireless networks in public places, be VERY careful about which networks you connect your devices. Also, when you're connected to these networks in public, never do anything on your device you wouldn't want the whole world watching.

A common hack that occurs is to set up a 'rogue access point' and acting as the man in the middle of your web use. Someone with a laptop computer can set up their own access point and steal your data.

Imagine you're sitting in an airport terminal in Chicago and you see "Chicago Free Wi-Fi". Sounds great right? You connect and use the internet to conduct your business. Depending on the sophistication of the hacker, anything you did online could have been watched and recorded. This can take place even if you think you're accessing a secure website, HTTPS URLs for instance.

Because of these risks, never connect to open wireless networks.

Use Two Factor Authentication

I debated for some time about including a section on two factor authentication. I'd like to include a small disclaimer that this information will not necessarily protect your device, but will help protect the data on your device. If you use your Google account for Gmail and as your primary email address, please consider enabling two factor authentication. The security of your Google account is a very important aspect of the security of your device as a whole.

To begin, let me describe two-factor authentication.
In the computer security realm, this is part of a concept called "Multifactor authentication". The idea is to use more than one form of identification to identity yourself to a computer system. The three types are "What you have", "What you know", and "What you are".

"What you have" is something you physically possess. For instance, if you work in a building that has magnetic locks that require a card swipe to gain access, the card is one factor of authentication.

"What you know" is a bit of information that can help identify yourself. To continue the example above, if you swipe your card to enter the building and a PIN or key code is required, that PIN or key code is something only you know and identifies yourself. Another example is a password or security question some accounts require you to enter such as 'Your first pet's name'.

"What you are" is most commonly called biometrics. The finger print reader on some phones or a palm or iris scan at the above door would be examples of this identification type.

What is multifactor authentication? It's using AT LEAST two of the above types of information. They must be from different categories; two different passwords (What you know) or two different key cards (What you have) would not be multifactor authentication.

While working for a government contractor for the Department of Defense, I encountered multifactor authentication on a daily basis. To enter our work area, we would need to scan our identification badge, then enter a PIN in the card reader. This combines "what you have" (the badge) with "what you know" (the PIN).

More and more I encounter companies that are using multifactor authentication to protect our accounts online. For example, banks often require you to prove your identity by receiving a text message or email before you can login to your account on a new computer.

 Text messages are not a good second factor authentication method because they are insecure. Learn more here: http://goo.gl/fm6qJk (Techcrunch.com)

Google's two factor authentication system is robust and can utilize a wide variety of different methods to secure your account. Google allows you to use any number of these security methods: Google's Authenticator Application, Voice or Text message to a specific phone number, backup codes, Google prompt and Security key.

Google Authenticator is a one-time password generating application that uses a shared secret password and/or the current time to authenticate your access. To set up the authenticator access, you use your device to 'scan' the QR code shown by Google. How to set up Google Authenticator is covered in the next section "Setup Authenticator and Prompt".

Voice or text message will either call you or send a text message with a code to enter when logging in. It's my recommendation to set this to a different phone than the one that has the authenticator application installed. If you lose your phone, you will have lost both the authenticator and the backup phone number for your account. Losing the authenticator and backup phone would make it very difficult to log in to your account and recover your access.

Google prompt will show you a "Yes or No" type popup on your device to allow your new logon. This would be an acceptable alternative to the Authenticator application above if you want a simpler way to log in. Rather than entering a code, you will just hit the Yes button that pops up on your device to log in. The setup of Google prompt is covered in the next section.

Backup codes are single-use 8 digit passcodes that would be required after entering your password. This is a good option to print and store somewhere secure, such as a safe, or to use when your phone is unavailable. This is most commonly used when traveling if you won't be able to use your device for Authenticator, Prompt or the voice/text messages.

The Security key is a small USB dongle that is plugged in to your computer, similar to a flash drive, that allows you to login to your account using Google's Chrome browser only. The requirement of using Chrome as your browser does limit this option to only computers where you have administrator rights. This will not work on public computers where you cannot install Google's Chrome browser.

Set Up Authenticator and Prompt

Authenticator and Google Prompt require the use of a desktop or laptop computer to complete the initial set up on the Google website. These options require that you have a lock screen setup on your device.

Visit the SMS/Voice setup page to enroll your account in 2-Step verification. http://accounts.google.com/SmsAuthConfig

After logging in to your Google account, follow the 2-step verification step-by-step procedure that is outlined on the web pages.

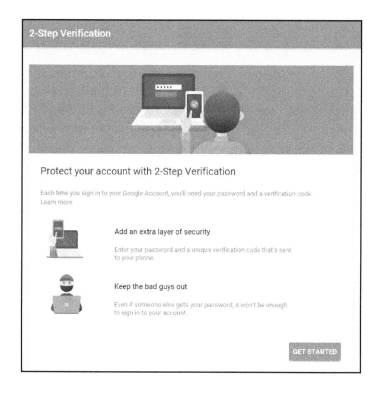

Set up a backup phone number that you can receive text messages or phone calls for the security codes.

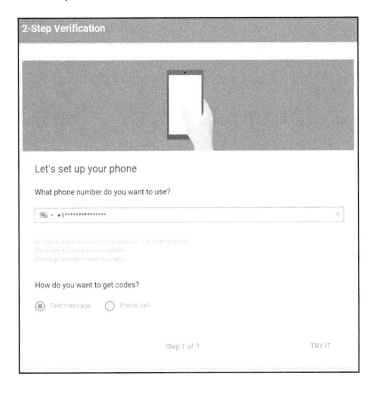

You will then receive a code via text message or phone call, which you will enter on the next screen.

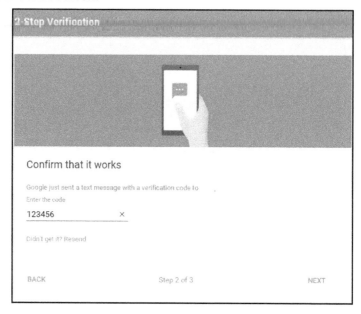

After you've confirmed the code, click *Turn on* to start your protection.

You will be taken to the main screen where you can select alternative second steps. I would advise using another option besides text message as your main secondary step.

Scroll to the *Set up alternative second step* section and leave that web browser open as we continue on to the next steps.

Google Authenticator

This application will generate a code that you will enter in the browser when you use your Google account on any 'new' device that you haven't used before. For example, if you visit a library or a friend's computer, it will prompt you for this security code. This code is your second factor authentication and is "What you have" by proving you have your Android device.

Download the Google Authenticator App to your Android phone or device. Visit the Google Play app store and search for "Google Authenticator". The icon looks like a metal G shown in the next screen shot to the left of the *Authenticator app*.

On your computer's web browser, scroll down to the 'alternative second step' section on the page below. The alternative second step page is located here: http://accounts.google.com/SmsAuthConfig

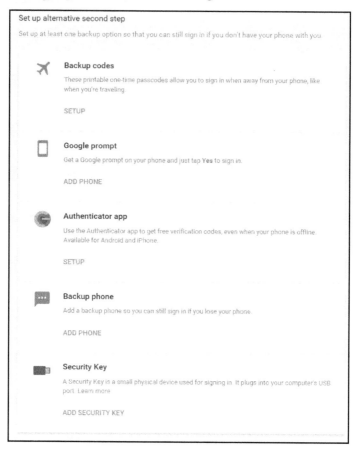

Click on *Setup*, under *Authenticator app.*

Select the type of phone you have and click next.
Open the Authenticator App on your Android Phone or Device, and select 'Set up account'. It will prompt you to scan the QR code on the screen.
To scan the code, you will need a barcode scanner app, which you will be directed to. If you don't want to install that app, select "Can't Scan it?" under the code on the computer.

If you can scan the code, you will be asked to enter the number generated by your Authenticator App on your Android device to the next screen on your computer. If you can't scan the code, select *Can't Scan it?* and you will have to enter the long series of numbers and letters from your computer to your device.

Your QR code will be much more complex than the one above. I have erased a majority of the code to hide the information it presented so you can't generate an authenticator for my account.

Complete! You've now set up the Authenticator App! It should roll the codes every 30 seconds or so and any new logins to your account will require this code.

Google Prompt

Google Prompt creates a pop-up on your Android device that allows you to tap 'yes' or 'no' regarding a new logon to your account. It's an alternative to the Authenticator and it also proves "What you have" by confirming you have your Android device. It may be easier to use than Authenticator and provides a similar security level.

From the web browser on your desktop or laptop computer, navigate back to the main 2-step verification page and find the alternative second step screen as shown below. (link http://accounts.google.com/SmsAuthConfig)

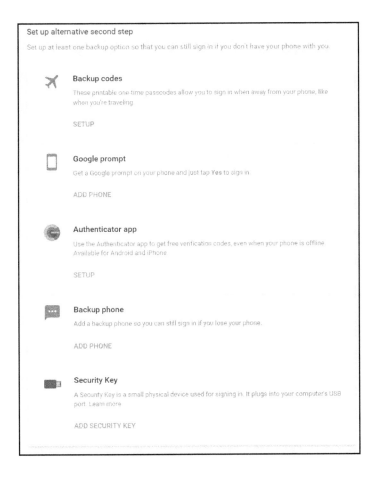

Click *Add Phone* under Google Prompt.

The website will ask which phone you would like to add. Select the make and model of the device you want to setup. Mine says "LG Nexus 5" and lists the other devices linked to my Google account. You must be logged in to your Google account on your device for it to appear in this list. If you can read your email in the Gmail App, then your account is set up. If your account is not set up, please add the account in *Settings, Accounts.*

You will next be sent a test prompt on your phone. Below is a screen shot from the web and app portion of the prompt.

Web (laptop or desktop) view:

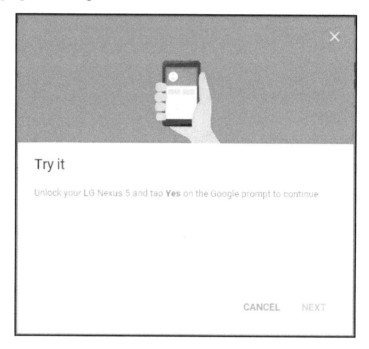

Application (Android device) view:

After you tap *Yes* on the phone, you're all set! Now when you attempt to log in to your Google account, you can select Google prompt as your second factor of authentication.

Thank you

Thank you for purchasing this book from the Keeping You Secure series. I hope this guide has helped you feel more secure in the use of your Android device. If there are any topics you would like to see in the future, please contact me through Amazon or on Goodreads. I hope to hear from you and look forward to the next in the series.

www.ingramcontent.com/pod-product-compliance
Lightning Source LLC
LaVergne TN
LVHW052315060326
832902LV00021B/3897